50 Farm-Fresh Egg Recipes for Home

By: Kelly Johnson

Table of Contents

- Classic Scrambled Eggs
- Perfect Poached Eggs
- Shakshuka (Poached Eggs in Tomato Sauce)
- Spinach and Feta Omelette
- Quiche Lorraine
- Deviled Eggs with Dill
- Egg Salad Sandwich
- Egg and Avocado Breakfast Toast
- Huevos Rancheros
- Spanish Tortilla (Potato Omelette)
- Baked Avocado Eggs
- Cloud Eggs with Parmesan
- Bacon and Egg Breakfast Muffins
- Soft-Boiled Eggs with Soldiers
- Ham and Cheese Egg Cups
- Egg Drop Soup
- Egg Casserole with Sausage and Cheese
- Simple Egg Fried Rice
- Poached Eggs on Avocado Toast
- Scrambled Eggs with Smoked Salmon
- Eggplant and Egg Stir-Fry
- Veggie Frittata
- Smoked Salmon Eggs Benedict
- Egg and Potato Hash
- Bacon-Wrapped Egg Cups
- Shredded Potato and Egg Skillet
- Spicy Egg Curry
- Mediterranean Eggplant and Egg Dish
- Scrambled Eggs with Mushrooms and Spinach
- Bacon and Egg Breakfast Burritos
- Japanese Tamago (Sweet Omelette)
- Sweet Potato and Egg Hash
- Soft-Boiled Eggs with Ramen
- Zucchini and Egg Scramble
- Breakfast Egg Tacos

- Cheesy Eggplant Parmesan
- Poached Eggs with Roasted Vegetables
- Deviled Eggs with Sriracha
- Egg and Bacon Pie
- Breakfast Quiche with Roasted Vegetables
- Shredded Brussels Sprouts with Poached Eggs
- Coddled Eggs in Creamy Spinach Sauce
- Lemon Herb Scrambled Eggs
- Chorizo and Egg Breakfast Burrito
- Tomato and Basil Omelette
- Sweet Corn and Egg Frittata
- Asparagus and Egg Salad
- Egg and Cheese Breakfast Sandwich
- Baked Eggs in Ham Cups
- Mushroom and Egg Breakfast Skillet

Classic Scrambled Eggs

Ingredients:

- 4 large eggs
- 2 tablespoons of butter
- Salt and pepper to taste
- Fresh herbs for garnish (optional)

Instructions:

1. Crack the eggs into a bowl, whisk them with a pinch of salt and pepper until well combined.
2. Heat the butter in a non-stick skillet over medium heat until melted.
3. Pour the eggs into the skillet and cook, stirring gently and continuously, for 3-4 minutes until the eggs are soft and creamy.
4. Serve immediately, garnished with fresh herbs if desired.

Perfect Poached Eggs

Ingredients:

- 2 large eggs
- 1 tablespoon of white vinegar
- Salt (optional)
- Pepper (optional)

Instructions:

1. Bring a pot of water to a gentle simmer, then add vinegar.
2. Crack each egg into a small bowl, then gently slide them into the simmering water.
3. Poach the eggs for about 3-4 minutes for runny yolks or longer for firmer yolks.
4. Remove the eggs with a slotted spoon, season with salt and pepper, and serve on toast or as desired.

Shakshuka (Poached Eggs in Tomato Sauce)

Ingredients:

- 2 tablespoons of olive oil
- 1 onion, chopped
- 1 bell pepper, chopped
- 2 cloves garlic, minced
- 1 can (14.5 oz) crushed tomatoes
- 1 teaspoon cumin
- 1 teaspoon paprika
- Salt and pepper to taste
- 4 large eggs
- Fresh cilantro for garnish

Instructions:

1. Heat olive oil in a skillet over medium heat. Add the onion, bell pepper, and garlic, cooking for 5 minutes until soft.
2. Add crushed tomatoes, cumin, paprika, salt, and pepper. Simmer for 10 minutes.
3. Make small wells in the tomato sauce and crack eggs into the wells. Cover and cook for 5-7 minutes until the eggs are cooked to your liking.
4. Garnish with fresh cilantro and serve with crusty bread.

Spinach and Feta Omelette

Ingredients:

- 3 large eggs
- 1/4 cup of fresh spinach, chopped
- 2 tablespoons of feta cheese, crumbled
- 1 tablespoon of olive oil
- Salt and pepper to taste

Instructions:

1. In a bowl, whisk the eggs with salt and pepper.
2. Heat olive oil in a skillet over medium heat. Add the spinach and cook for 1-2 minutes until wilted.
3. Pour the eggs into the skillet and cook for 2-3 minutes until the edges start to set.
4. Sprinkle feta cheese on top and fold the omelette in half. Cook for another 1-2 minutes until fully set.
5. Serve immediately.

Quiche Lorraine

Ingredients:

- 1 pre-made pie crust
- 6 large eggs
- 1 cup of heavy cream
- 1/2 cup of grated Swiss cheese
- 1/2 cup of cooked bacon, crumbled
- 1/2 cup of sautéed onions
- Salt and pepper to taste

Instructions:

1. Preheat the oven to 375°F (190°C). In a bowl, whisk together eggs, heavy cream, salt, and pepper.
2. Add the grated Swiss cheese, crumbled bacon, and sautéed onions to the egg mixture.
3. Pour the mixture into the pie crust and bake for 30-40 minutes until set and golden on top.
4. Let cool for a few minutes before slicing and serving.

Deviled Eggs with Dill

Ingredients:

- 6 hard-boiled eggs, peeled and halved
- 3 tablespoons of mayonnaise
- 1 teaspoon of Dijon mustard
- 1 teaspoon of white vinegar
- Salt and pepper to taste
- Fresh dill for garnish

Instructions:

1. Scoop the yolks from the hard-boiled eggs into a bowl.
2. Mash the yolks with mayonnaise, Dijon mustard, white vinegar, salt, and pepper.
3. Spoon or pipe the mixture back into the egg whites.
4. Garnish with fresh dill and serve chilled.

Egg Salad Sandwich

Ingredients:

- 4 hard-boiled eggs, chopped
- 2 tablespoons of mayonnaise
- 1 teaspoon of Dijon mustard
- 1 tablespoon of fresh chives, chopped
- Salt and pepper to taste
- 4 slices of bread

Instructions:

1. In a bowl, mix the chopped eggs with mayonnaise, Dijon mustard, chives, salt, and pepper.
2. Spread the egg salad mixture between two slices of bread.
3. Serve with a side salad or chips.

Egg and Avocado Breakfast Toast

Ingredients:

- 2 slices of whole-grain bread, toasted
- 1 ripe avocado, mashed
- 2 large eggs, cooked to your preference (fried, poached, or scrambled)
- Salt and pepper to taste
- Red pepper flakes for garnish

Instructions:

1. Spread mashed avocado on the toasted bread.
2. Top with the cooked eggs and season with salt and pepper.
3. Garnish with red pepper flakes and serve immediately.

Huevos Rancheros

Ingredients:

- 2 large eggs
- 2 corn tortillas
- 1/2 cup of salsa
- 1/4 cup of black beans, heated
- 1/4 cup of shredded cheese
- Fresh cilantro for garnish

Instructions:

1. Heat the corn tortillas in a skillet until lightly crispy.
2. In a separate skillet, cook the eggs to your liking.
3. Place the tortillas on a plate and top with salsa, black beans, cooked eggs, and shredded cheese.
4. Garnish with fresh cilantro and serve immediately.

Spanish Tortilla (Potato Omelette)

Ingredients:

- 4 large eggs
- 3 medium potatoes, peeled and sliced
- 1 onion, sliced
- 1/4 cup of olive oil
- Salt and pepper to taste

Instructions:

1. Heat olive oil in a skillet over medium heat. Add the sliced potatoes and onion, cooking until tender, about 10 minutes.
2. In a bowl, whisk the eggs with salt and pepper. Add the cooked potatoes and onions to the egg mixture.
3. Pour the mixture back into the skillet and cook on low heat for 5-7 minutes, until the eggs are set.
4. Flip the tortilla onto a plate and cook the other side for another 3-4 minutes.
5. Let cool slightly before slicing and serving.

Baked Avocado Eggs

Ingredients:

- 2 ripe avocados, halved and pitted
- 4 large eggs
- Salt and pepper to taste
- Red pepper flakes (optional)

Instructions:

1. Preheat the oven to 425°F (220°C).
2. Scoop out a little extra avocado from each half to create room for the egg.
3. Place the avocado halves in a baking dish. Crack an egg into each half.
4. Season with salt, pepper, and red pepper flakes if desired.
5. Bake for 12-15 minutes, or until the egg whites are set but the yolk is still runny.
6. Serve immediately, garnished with fresh herbs or a sprinkle of cheese.

Cloud Eggs with Parmesan

Ingredients:

- 4 large eggs
- 2 tablespoons of grated Parmesan cheese
- Salt and pepper to taste
- Fresh herbs for garnish

Instructions:

1. Preheat the oven to 375°F (190°C). Line a baking sheet with parchment paper.
2. Separate the egg whites from the yolks, placing the whites in a bowl and the yolks in separate small bowls.
3. Whisk the egg whites until stiff peaks form, then gently fold in the grated Parmesan cheese.
4. Spoon the whipped egg whites onto the baking sheet, creating little nests. Make an indent in the center of each.
5. Carefully place a yolk in each indent.
6. Bake for 5-7 minutes, or until the whites are golden and set.
7. Serve immediately with a sprinkle of fresh herbs.

Bacon and Egg Breakfast Muffins

Ingredients:

- 6 large eggs
- 6 slices of cooked bacon, crumbled
- 1 cup of shredded cheese (cheddar or your choice)
- 1/2 cup of milk
- Salt and pepper to taste
- 6 English muffin halves

Instructions:

1. Preheat the oven to 350°F (175°C) and lightly grease a muffin tin.
2. Toast the English muffin halves and place them in the bottom of each muffin tin cup.
3. Whisk the eggs, milk, salt, and pepper together, then stir in the crumbled bacon and shredded cheese.
4. Pour the egg mixture over the muffin halves.
5. Bake for 15-18 minutes until the eggs are set and golden.
6. Let cool slightly before serving.

Soft-Boiled Eggs with Soldiers

Ingredients:

- 4 large eggs
- 4 slices of whole-grain or white bread
- Salt and pepper to taste

Instructions:

1. Bring a pot of water to a boil. Lower the eggs into the water and cook for 4-5 minutes for soft-boiled eggs with runny yolks.
2. While the eggs are cooking, toast the bread and cut it into long strips (soldiers).
3. Once the eggs are done, remove them from the water and let cool slightly.
4. Serve the eggs in egg cups with soldiers for dipping. Season with salt and pepper.

Ham and Cheese Egg Cups

Ingredients:

- 6 slices of ham
- 6 large eggs
- 1/2 cup of shredded cheese (Swiss or cheddar)
- Salt and pepper to taste

Instructions:

1. Preheat the oven to 375°F (190°C).
2. Line a muffin tin with ham slices, creating a cup shape.
3. Crack an egg into each ham cup and sprinkle with shredded cheese, salt, and pepper.
4. Bake for 12-15 minutes or until the eggs are set to your liking.
5. Serve warm with toast or a side of vegetables.

Egg Drop Soup

Ingredients:

- 4 cups of chicken broth
- 2 large eggs
- 1 tablespoon of soy sauce
- 1 teaspoon of sesame oil
- 1/4 teaspoon of ginger, minced
- Green onions, sliced for garnish

Instructions:

1. Heat the chicken broth in a pot over medium heat. Add the soy sauce, sesame oil, and minced ginger.
2. In a separate bowl, beat the eggs.
3. Bring the broth to a gentle simmer and slowly pour the beaten eggs into the broth in a thin stream, stirring gently to create egg ribbons.
4. Let cook for 1-2 minutes, then serve immediately, garnished with green onions.

Egg Casserole with Sausage and Cheese

Ingredients:

- 6 large eggs
- 1 cup of milk
- 1/2 pound of breakfast sausage, cooked and crumbled
- 1 cup of shredded cheddar cheese
- 1/2 teaspoon of garlic powder
- Salt and pepper to taste

Instructions:

1. Preheat the oven to 350°F (175°C) and grease a baking dish.
2. In a bowl, whisk together the eggs, milk, garlic powder, salt, and pepper.
3. Stir in the cooked sausage and shredded cheese.
4. Pour the mixture into the greased baking dish and bake for 25-30 minutes until the eggs are set and golden on top.
5. Let cool slightly before slicing and serving.

Simple Egg Fried Rice

Ingredients:

- 2 cups of cooked rice (preferably day-old)
- 2 large eggs, scrambled
- 1/2 cup of frozen peas and carrots
- 2 tablespoons of soy sauce
- 1 tablespoon of sesame oil
- Green onions for garnish

Instructions:

1. Heat sesame oil in a large skillet or wok over medium heat. Add the frozen peas and carrots and cook for 2-3 minutes.
2. Push the vegetables to the side and scramble the eggs in the skillet.
3. Add the cooked rice to the skillet, stirring to combine with the eggs and vegetables.
4. Pour soy sauce over the rice and cook for another 3-4 minutes, stirring constantly.
5. Serve warm, garnished with sliced green onions.

Poached Eggs on Avocado Toast

Ingredients:

- 2 large eggs
- 2 slices of whole-grain bread, toasted
- 1 ripe avocado, mashed
- Salt and pepper to taste
- Red pepper flakes (optional)

Instructions:

1. Bring a pot of water to a gentle simmer and add a splash of vinegar.
2. Crack the eggs into the simmering water and poach for 3-4 minutes, or until the whites are set but the yolks are runny.
3. While the eggs are cooking, spread mashed avocado on the toasted bread.
4. Top with the poached eggs, season with salt and pepper, and sprinkle with red pepper flakes if desired.
5. Serve immediately.

Scrambled Eggs with Smoked Salmon

Ingredients:

- 4 large eggs
- 2 oz smoked salmon, torn into pieces
- 1 tablespoon butter
- Salt and pepper to taste
- Fresh dill for garnish

Instructions:

1. Crack the eggs into a bowl and whisk until smooth. Season with salt and pepper.
2. Heat the butter in a non-stick pan over medium heat. Pour in the eggs and cook, stirring constantly, until they begin to set but are still slightly runny.
3. Gently fold in the smoked salmon and cook for an additional 1-2 minutes.
4. Garnish with fresh dill and serve immediately with toast or crackers.

Eggplant and Egg Stir-Fry

Ingredients:

- 1 medium eggplant, diced
- 4 large eggs, beaten
- 1 tablespoon soy sauce
- 1 tablespoon sesame oil
- 2 cloves garlic, minced
- 1 teaspoon ginger, minced
- 1/2 onion, sliced
- Salt and pepper to taste
- Green onions for garnish

Instructions:

1. Heat sesame oil in a large pan over medium heat. Add the garlic, ginger, and onion, and sauté for 2-3 minutes until softened.
2. Add the diced eggplant and cook for 5-7 minutes, stirring occasionally until softened.
3. Push the eggplant mixture to the side and pour in the beaten eggs, scrambling them until cooked through.
4. Stir everything together and season with soy sauce, salt, and pepper.
5. Garnish with green onions and serve.

Veggie Frittata

Ingredients:

- 6 large eggs
- 1/2 cup milk
- 1/2 cup bell peppers, diced
- 1/2 cup spinach, chopped
- 1/4 cup onions, diced
- 1/2 cup feta cheese, crumbled
- Salt and pepper to taste

Instructions:

1. Preheat the oven to 375°F (190°C).
2. In a large oven-safe skillet, sauté the onions and bell peppers in a little oil over medium heat for 3-4 minutes until soft.
3. Add the spinach and cook until wilted.
4. In a separate bowl, whisk together the eggs, milk, salt, and pepper. Pour the egg mixture over the veggies.
5. Sprinkle crumbled feta on top and transfer the skillet to the oven.
6. Bake for 15-20 minutes or until the eggs are set. Slice and serve.

Smoked Salmon Eggs Benedict

Ingredients:

- 4 large eggs
- 4 English muffin halves, toasted
- 4 slices smoked salmon
- 1 tablespoon vinegar
- Hollandaise sauce (store-bought or homemade)

Instructions:

1. Bring a pot of water to a gentle simmer, add vinegar. Crack the eggs into the simmering water and poach for 3-4 minutes.
2. Place a slice of smoked salmon on each toasted English muffin half.
3. Once the eggs are poached, carefully place one egg on top of each muffin half with salmon.
4. Spoon hollandaise sauce over the eggs and serve immediately.

Egg and Potato Hash

Ingredients:

- 2 large potatoes, diced
- 4 large eggs
- 1/2 cup onion, diced
- 1/2 bell pepper, diced
- 2 tablespoons olive oil
- Salt and pepper to taste

Instructions:

1. Heat olive oil in a large skillet over medium heat. Add the potatoes and cook for 10-12 minutes, stirring occasionally until golden and tender.
2. Add the onion and bell pepper and cook for another 5 minutes until softened.
3. Create small wells in the hash and crack an egg into each. Cover and cook for 5-7 minutes, until the eggs are cooked to your liking.
4. Season with salt and pepper and serve warm.

Bacon-Wrapped Egg Cups

Ingredients:

- 6 slices of bacon
- 6 large eggs
- Salt and pepper to taste
- Fresh herbs for garnish (optional)

Instructions:

1. Preheat the oven to 375°F (190°C).
2. Line the edges of a muffin tin with the bacon slices, creating a cup shape.
3. Crack an egg into each bacon cup and season with salt and pepper.
4. Bake for 12-15 minutes, or until the eggs are set.
5. Garnish with fresh herbs and serve immediately.

Shredded Potato and Egg Skillet

Ingredients:

- 2 large potatoes, shredded
- 4 large eggs
- 1 tablespoon olive oil
- 1/4 cup onion, diced
- 1/2 teaspoon paprika
- Salt and pepper to taste

Instructions:

1. Heat olive oil in a large skillet over medium heat. Add the diced onion and cook for 2-3 minutes until soft.
2. Add the shredded potatoes and cook for 10-12 minutes, stirring occasionally, until crispy and golden.
3. Season with paprika, salt, and pepper.
4. Create small wells in the potatoes and crack an egg into each. Cover and cook for 5-7 minutes until the eggs are set.
5. Serve warm with extra seasoning if desired.

Spicy Egg Curry

Ingredients:

- 6 large eggs, hard-boiled
- 1 tablespoon vegetable oil
- 1 onion, diced
- 2 cloves garlic, minced
- 1 tablespoon ginger, minced
- 1 teaspoon curry powder
- 1/2 teaspoon turmeric
- 1/2 cup crushed tomatoes
- 1/2 cup coconut milk
- Fresh cilantro for garnish
- Salt and pepper to taste

Instructions:

1. Heat vegetable oil in a pan over medium heat. Add the onion, garlic, and ginger, and sauté until softened.
2. Stir in the curry powder and turmeric and cook for 1 minute.
3. Add the crushed tomatoes and coconut milk. Simmer for 5-7 minutes until the sauce thickens.
4. Cut the hard-boiled eggs in half and gently add them to the curry sauce.
5. Cook for an additional 2-3 minutes and season with salt and pepper.
6. Garnish with fresh cilantro and serve with rice or naan.

Mediterranean Eggplant and Egg Dish

Ingredients:

- 1 medium eggplant, sliced
- 4 large eggs
- 1/4 cup olive oil
- 2 cloves garlic, minced
- 1/2 cup tomatoes, diced
- 1 teaspoon oregano
- Salt and pepper to taste
- Feta cheese for garnish

Instructions:

1. Preheat the oven to 375°F (190°C). Place the eggplant slices on a baking sheet and drizzle with olive oil.
2. Roast the eggplant for 20-25 minutes, flipping halfway, until tender and golden.
3. In a pan, sauté garlic in olive oil for 2 minutes, then add the diced tomatoes and oregano. Cook for 5 minutes, stirring occasionally.
4. Create wells in the tomato mixture and crack eggs into each.
5. Cover and cook until the eggs are set. Season with salt and pepper.
6. Garnish with feta cheese and serve warm.

Scrambled Eggs with Mushrooms and Spinach

Ingredients:

- 4 large eggs
- 1 cup mushrooms, sliced
- 1/2 cup spinach, chopped
- 1 tablespoon butter
- Salt and pepper to taste

Instructions:

1. Heat butter in a pan over medium heat. Add the mushrooms and cook for 5-7 minutes until soft.
2. Add the spinach and cook for 2-3 minutes until wilted.
3. Crack the eggs into a bowl, whisk, and pour into the pan. Scramble the eggs with the mushrooms and spinach until cooked through.
4. Season with salt and pepper and serve immediately.

Bacon and Egg Breakfast Burritos

Ingredients:

- 4 large eggs
- 4 flour tortillas
- 4 slices of bacon, cooked and crumbled
- 1/2 cup shredded cheddar cheese
- 1/4 cup salsa
- 1/4 cup avocado, mashed
- Salt and pepper to taste

Instructions:

1. Scramble the eggs in a pan over medium heat until fully cooked. Season with salt and pepper.
2. Warm the tortillas and spread mashed avocado on each.
3. Add scrambled eggs, crumbled bacon, shredded cheese, and a spoonful of salsa.
4. Roll up the tortillas into burritos, folding in the sides as you go.
5. Serve immediately and enjoy!

Japanese Tamago (Sweet Omelette)

Ingredients:

- 4 large eggs
- 2 tablespoons soy sauce
- 1 tablespoon sugar
- 1 tablespoon mirin (optional)
- 1 teaspoon vegetable oil

Instructions:

1. In a bowl, whisk together the eggs, soy sauce, sugar, and mirin until smooth.
2. Heat a small amount of oil in a rectangular or square pan over medium heat.
3. Pour a small amount of the egg mixture into the pan, swirling to cover the bottom.
4. Once it starts to set, roll the omelette towards you, then push it to the side of the pan.
5. Pour more egg mixture into the pan and lift the rolled omelette to let the liquid flow underneath.
6. Continue this process until all the egg mixture is used up. Slice the omelette and serve warm.

Sweet Potato and Egg Hash

Ingredients:

- 2 medium sweet potatoes, peeled and diced
- 4 large eggs
- 1 tablespoon olive oil
- 1/2 onion, diced
- 1/2 red bell pepper, diced
- Salt and pepper to taste

Instructions:

1. Heat olive oil in a large skillet over medium heat. Add the sweet potatoes and cook for 8-10 minutes, stirring occasionally, until tender and lightly browned.
2. Add the diced onion and bell pepper, cooking for an additional 3-4 minutes until softened.
3. Make small wells in the hash and crack an egg into each.
4. Cover the pan and cook until the eggs are set. Season with salt and pepper, then serve.

Soft-Boiled Eggs with Ramen

Ingredients:

- 2 large eggs
- 1 pack of ramen noodles
- 1 tablespoon soy sauce
- 1 teaspoon sesame oil
- Green onions for garnish
- Nori (seaweed) strips (optional)

Instructions:

1. Bring a pot of water to a boil. Add the eggs and cook for 7 minutes for soft-boiled eggs.
2. Remove the eggs and place them in cold water to stop the cooking process. Peel and set aside.
3. Cook the ramen noodles according to package instructions. Once cooked, drain and set aside.
4. In a bowl, combine the soy sauce and sesame oil. Add the cooked ramen noodles and toss to coat.
5. Halve the soft-boiled eggs and place them on top of the noodles. Garnish with green onions and nori. Serve warm.

Zucchini and Egg Scramble

Ingredients:

- 4 large eggs
- 1 zucchini, grated
- 1/2 onion, diced
- 1 tablespoon olive oil
- Salt and pepper to taste
- Fresh herbs for garnish (optional)

Instructions:

1. Heat olive oil in a pan over medium heat. Add the diced onion and cook for 2-3 minutes until softened.
2. Add the grated zucchini and cook for 4-5 minutes, until softened and water is released.
3. Crack the eggs into the pan and scramble with the zucchini mixture until fully cooked.
4. Season with salt and pepper, then garnish with fresh herbs if desired. Serve immediately.

Breakfast Egg Tacos

Ingredients:

- 4 large eggs
- 4 small corn tortillas
- 1/4 cup shredded cheese
- 1/4 cup salsa
- 1/4 cup avocado, sliced
- 1 tablespoon sour cream (optional)
- Salt and pepper to taste

Instructions:

1. Scramble the eggs in a pan over medium heat, seasoning with salt and pepper.
2. Warm the tortillas and layer each with scrambled eggs, shredded cheese, salsa, and avocado.
3. Top with a dollop of sour cream if desired.
4. Fold the tortillas into tacos and serve immediately.

Cheesy Eggplant Parmesan

Ingredients:

- 2 large eggplants, sliced into rounds
- 4 large eggs, beaten
- 1 cup breadcrumbs
- 1/2 cup grated Parmesan cheese
- 1 cup marinara sauce
- 1 cup shredded mozzarella cheese
- Salt and pepper to taste
- Olive oil for frying

Instructions:

1. Preheat the oven to 375°F (190°C).
2. Dip the eggplant slices in the beaten eggs, then coat them in breadcrumbs and Parmesan cheese.
3. Heat olive oil in a pan over medium heat and fry the eggplant slices until golden on both sides.
4. Place the fried eggplant slices on a baking sheet, spoon marinara sauce over them, and top with mozzarella cheese.
5. Bake in the oven for 10-12 minutes until the cheese is melted and bubbly. Serve warm.

Poached Eggs with Roasted Vegetables

Ingredients:

- 4 large eggs
- 1 cup mixed vegetables (e.g., carrots, zucchini, bell peppers)
- 1 tablespoon olive oil
- Salt and pepper to taste
- Fresh parsley for garnish

Instructions:

1. Preheat the oven to 400°F (200°C).
2. Toss the mixed vegetables in olive oil, salt, and pepper, and roast in the oven for 20-25 minutes until tender.
3. Meanwhile, bring a pot of water to a gentle simmer. Poach the eggs for 3-4 minutes until the whites are set but the yolks are still runny.
4. Serve the poached eggs on top of the roasted vegetables and garnish with fresh parsley.

Deviled Eggs with Sriracha

Ingredients:

- 6 large eggs, hard-boiled and halved
- 1/4 cup mayonnaise
- 1 tablespoon Dijon mustard
- 1 teaspoon Sriracha sauce (adjust to taste)
- 1 teaspoon white vinegar
- Salt and pepper to taste
- Paprika for garnish

Instructions:

1. Scoop the yolks out of the hard-boiled eggs and place them in a bowl.
2. Mash the yolks and mix with mayonnaise, mustard, Sriracha sauce, white vinegar, salt, and pepper.
3. Spoon the filling into the egg whites or pipe it using a pastry bag.
4. Garnish with paprika and serve chilled.

Egg and Bacon Pie

Ingredients:

- 4 large eggs
- 6 slices of bacon, cooked and crumbled
- 1 cup heavy cream
- 1 pre-made pie crust
- 1/2 cup shredded cheddar cheese
- Salt and pepper to taste
- Fresh herbs for garnish (optional)

Instructions:

1. Preheat your oven to 375°F (190°C).
2. In a bowl, whisk together the eggs, cream, salt, and pepper.
3. Place the cooked bacon in the pie crust and sprinkle with shredded cheddar cheese.
4. Pour the egg mixture over the bacon and cheese, spreading evenly.
5. Bake for 25-30 minutes or until the eggs are set and golden on top.
6. Let cool slightly before slicing. Garnish with fresh herbs if desired.

Breakfast Quiche with Roasted Vegetables

Ingredients:

- 4 large eggs
- 1 pre-made pie crust
- 1 cup mixed roasted vegetables (e.g., bell peppers, zucchini, onions)
- 1/2 cup shredded cheese (cheddar or mozzarella)
- 1/2 cup milk or cream
- Salt and pepper to taste
- Fresh herbs for garnish (optional)

Instructions:

1. Preheat your oven to 375°F (190°C).
2. Whisk together eggs, milk, salt, and pepper in a bowl.
3. Arrange the roasted vegetables evenly in the pie crust and sprinkle with cheese.
4. Pour the egg mixture over the vegetables and cheese, spreading evenly.
5. Bake for 25-30 minutes, or until the quiche is set and lightly golden on top.
6. Allow it to cool slightly before slicing. Garnish with fresh herbs if desired.

Shredded Brussels Sprouts with Poached Eggs

Ingredients:

- 4 large eggs
- 2 cups Brussels sprouts, shredded
- 1 tablespoon olive oil
- 2 cloves garlic, minced
- Salt and pepper to taste
- Fresh lemon juice (optional)

Instructions:

1. Heat olive oil in a large skillet over medium heat. Add garlic and sauté for 1-2 minutes.
2. Add the shredded Brussels sprouts and cook, stirring occasionally, for 8-10 minutes until softened and slightly crispy.
3. Meanwhile, bring a pot of water to a simmer and poach the eggs for 3-4 minutes.
4. Season the Brussels sprouts with salt, pepper, and a squeeze of fresh lemon juice (optional).
5. Serve the poached eggs over the Brussels sprouts and enjoy!

Coddled Eggs in Creamy Spinach Sauce

Ingredients:

- 4 large eggs
- 2 cups fresh spinach, chopped
- 1/2 cup heavy cream
- 1 tablespoon butter
- Salt and pepper to taste
- Fresh grated Parmesan cheese (optional)

Instructions:

1. Bring a pot of water to a gentle simmer and add the eggs. Coddle the eggs by simmering them for 3-4 minutes.
2. Meanwhile, heat butter in a pan over medium heat. Add chopped spinach and cook for 2-3 minutes until wilted.
3. Add heavy cream to the spinach, stirring until the sauce is smooth. Season with salt and pepper.
4. Serve the coddled eggs over the creamy spinach sauce. Garnish with grated Parmesan cheese if desired.

Lemon Herb Scrambled Eggs

Ingredients:

- 4 large eggs
- 1 tablespoon butter
- 1 tablespoon fresh herbs (such as parsley, chives, or thyme), chopped
- Zest of 1 lemon
- Salt and pepper to taste

Instructions:

1. In a bowl, whisk together the eggs, fresh herbs, lemon zest, salt, and pepper.
2. Heat butter in a skillet over medium-low heat.
3. Pour the egg mixture into the pan and cook gently, stirring occasionally, until scrambled and creamy.
4. Serve warm, garnished with additional fresh herbs and a squeeze of lemon juice if desired.

Chorizo and Egg Breakfast Burrito

Ingredients:

- 4 large eggs
- 1/2 pound chorizo sausage, crumbled and cooked
- 4 flour tortillas
- 1/2 cup shredded cheese (cheddar or Monterey Jack)
- 1/4 cup salsa
- 1/4 cup avocado, mashed
- Fresh cilantro for garnish

Instructions:

1. Scramble the eggs in a pan over medium heat, seasoning with salt and pepper.
2. Warm the tortillas and spread mashed avocado on each.
3. Add scrambled eggs, cooked chorizo, and shredded cheese to the tortillas.
4. Top with salsa and roll the tortillas into burritos, folding in the sides.
5. Serve immediately, garnished with fresh cilantro.

Tomato and Basil Omelette

Ingredients:

- 3 large eggs
- 1/4 cup fresh basil, chopped
- 1/2 cup cherry tomatoes, halved
- 1 tablespoon olive oil
- Salt and pepper to taste
- Grated Parmesan cheese (optional)

Instructions:

1. Heat olive oil in a skillet over medium heat.
2. Whisk together eggs, salt, and pepper. Pour into the skillet and cook for 1-2 minutes.
3. Add halved tomatoes and chopped basil to one half of the omelette.
4. Fold the omelette over and cook for another 1-2 minutes until the eggs are fully set.
5. Optionally, sprinkle with grated Parmesan cheese and serve.

Sweet Corn and Egg Frittata

Ingredients:

- 6 large eggs
- 1 cup sweet corn kernels (fresh or frozen)
- 1/2 cup diced bell pepper
- 1/2 cup diced onion
- 1/2 cup shredded cheese (cheddar or mozzarella)
- 1 tablespoon olive oil
- Salt and pepper to taste

Instructions:

1. Preheat your oven to 375°F (190°C).
2. Heat olive oil in an oven-safe skillet over medium heat. Add diced onion and bell pepper, sautéing for 5 minutes.
3. Stir in sweet corn and cook for another 2 minutes.
4. Whisk together eggs, salt, and pepper. Pour over the vegetables and top with shredded cheese.
5. Transfer the skillet to the oven and bake for 10-12 minutes until the frittata is set and golden on top.
6. Slice and serve warm.

Asparagus and Egg Salad

Ingredients:

- 4 large eggs
- 1 bunch asparagus, trimmed and steamed
- 1 tablespoon olive oil
- 1 tablespoon Dijon mustard
- 1 teaspoon white wine vinegar
- Salt and pepper to taste
- Fresh parsley for garnish

Instructions:

1. Hard boil the eggs by placing them in a pot of water, bringing it to a boil, and then simmering for 10 minutes. Peel and chop.
2. Steam the asparagus until tender and chop into bite-sized pieces.
3. In a bowl, whisk together olive oil, Dijon mustard, white wine vinegar, salt, and pepper to make the dressing.
4. Toss the chopped eggs and asparagus with the dressing.
5. Garnish with fresh parsley and serve chilled.

Egg and Cheese Breakfast Sandwich

Ingredients:

- 2 large eggs
- 2 slices of bread (your choice)
- 2 slices of cheese (cheddar, Swiss, or American)
- 1 tablespoon butter
- Salt and pepper to taste
- Optional: spinach, tomato, or avocado slices

Instructions:

1. Toast the bread slices and butter them on one side.
2. In a skillet, cook eggs to your preference (scrambled, fried, or poached) and season with salt and pepper.
3. Place a slice of cheese on one egg while it's still hot to melt.
4. Assemble the sandwich by placing the egg and cheese on one slice of bread. Add optional toppings like spinach, tomato, or avocado if desired.
5. Top with the second slice of bread and serve immediately.

Baked Eggs in Ham Cups

Ingredients:

- 4 slices of ham
- 4 large eggs
- 1/4 cup shredded cheese (optional)
- Salt and pepper to taste
- Fresh herbs for garnish (optional)

Instructions:

1. Preheat your oven to 375°F (190°C).
2. Grease a muffin tin and line each cup with a slice of ham.
3. Crack one egg into each ham cup and season with salt and pepper.
4. Optionally, sprinkle with shredded cheese.
5. Bake for 12-15 minutes, or until the eggs are set to your liking.
6. Garnish with fresh herbs and serve.

Mushroom and Egg Breakfast Skillet

Ingredients:

- 2 large eggs
- 1 cup mushrooms, sliced
- 1/4 cup onion, diced
- 1 tablespoon olive oil
- 1/2 teaspoon garlic powder
- Salt and pepper to taste
- Fresh herbs for garnish (optional)

Instructions:

1. Heat olive oil in a skillet over medium heat. Add the diced onion and sauté for 3-4 minutes.
2. Add the sliced mushrooms and cook for 5-6 minutes until tender.
3. Crack the eggs over the vegetables and season with garlic powder, salt, and pepper.
4. Cover the skillet and cook for 4-5 minutes until the eggs are set, or cook longer for firmer eggs.
5. Garnish with fresh herbs and serve warm.